Elizabethan England

The England of the 1580s was already well on the way to becoming a world power—a thrusting, forward-looking society with an expanding economy and a growing sense of self-confident nationhood. After the painful upheavals of the great mid-century social, political and spiritual revolution, conveniently known as the English Reformation, the vast majority of the islanders were united within the framework of a middle-of-the-road Protestant national church and living at peace under the rule of their much-loved and respected Queen. All those sceptics who had once cast doubts on the ability of an unmarried woman to govern the country had long since been confounded. In 1588 Elizabeth Tudor celebrated the thirtieth anniversary of her accession and could point to a record of personal and political achievement unmatched by any of her fellow monarchs.

By the 1580s the romantic cult of the Queen as Gloriana was reaching its height. Looking back across the centuries this popular veneration of Elizabeth as a cross between Protestant saint and classical goddess may sometimes seem more than a little absurd, but to the Elizabethans themselves, brought up as they were on the Bible and the classics, it seemed quite natural. Elizabeth I, it has been said, represented England as no other ruler ever did and her lifelong love affair with her subjects remains one of the wonders of the age. 'She is very much wedded to the people and thinks as they do,' commented the Spanish ambassador in the first year of her reign, and from the very beginning Elizabeth set out to win the hearts of 'all her husbands, the good people of England,' telling them on every available opportunity that while they might have many greater princes to rule over them, they would never have one that loved them better.

Every year the Queen travelled for many hundreds of miles over shockingly bad roads on her famous summer progresses in order to see and be seen by as many of her people as possible. During the course of these journeys she would receive hundreds of loyal addresses delivered by nervous civic dignitaries, sit through hundreds of amateur plays and pageants staged for her entertainment, and listen patiently to endless sermons and Latin disputations. Always smiling, always appreciative, always approachable and ready to listen to the complaints of the afflicted, she would personally accept and read petitions from the meanest rustics, assuring them that she would 'take a particular care of their affairs' and would always be as good as her word. She was never seen angry or offended with the most uncouth or importunate supplicant and never missed a chance of making a gracious gesture or performing some small act of kindness. Everywhere she went Elizabeth was greeted with 'great acclamations and signs of joy,' to which she responded by ordering her carriage to be taken where the crowds seemed thickest and standing up to thank the people.

Foreign visitors, especially the Germans and Italians, were impressed by the wealth and productivity of the land the Queen journeyed through. The rolling pastures of the Cotswold uplands and the fertile Midland plain supported

Queen Elizabeth as 'empress,' her feet planted on a map of England. The portrait is believed to have been commissioned to commemorate the Queen's visit to Sir Henry Lee at Ditchley in Oxfordshire in 1592

huge flocks of sheep on whose broad woolly backs much of England's economic prosperity rested. Fat cattle grazed in the water meadows which bordered wide, slow-flowing rivers teeming with fish and waterfowl; great tracts of virgin forest were alive with deer and other game, while the fields and orchards of southern England from Kent to Devon and Hereford yielded such bountiful crops that to continental eyes the islanders lived almost indecently well.

Certainly life was becoming steadily more comfortable for many of the Queen's subjects. More and more yeomen's houses were being built with chimneys, or having chimneys added, to carry off the smoke of the cooking fire, and with parlours—rooms purely for show. A contemporary observer of the social scene also commented that the use of glass was increasing in farmhouse windows, previously filled with panels of horn or wooden lattice, and that feather beds and pillows, once regarded as luxuries fit only for women in childbed, were now beginning to come into general use.

London

Elizabethan England was a predominantly agricultural society—about four-fifths of the people lived on and by the land—and compared with Italy, for example, English towns were few and small. The exception was London, 'the flower of cities all' as the poet William Dunbar described it. London was huge, the biggest capital city in Europe, with a population of more than 100 000 and still growing. A Swiss visitor, Thomas Platter of Basle, wrote: 'This city of London is so large and splendidly built, so populous and excellent in crafts and merchant citizens, and so prosperous, that it is not only the first in the whole realm of England, but is esteemed one of the most famous in all Christendom.' Another visitor, who came over to England with the Duke of Wirtemberg in the early 1590s, also spoke of London with admiration as 'a large, excellent and mighty city of business,' where most of the inhabitants were engaged in buying and selling merchandise and trading in every corner of the world. 'It is a very populous city,' he went on, 'so that one can scarcely pass along the streets on account of the throng.' The citizens and their wives were all 'magnificently apparelled,' but they were a proud, overbearing lot. 'They care little for foreigners, but scoff and laugh at them.'

London had its traffic problems even then. 'The number of drays, carts and coaches, more than hath been accustomed, the streets and lanes being straitened [narrow] , must needs be dangerous, as daily experience proveth,' wrote John Stow, tailor, historian and author of the *Survey of London*. 'By the good laws and customs of this city, shod carts are forbidden to enter, except upon reasonable cause ... also the fore horse of every carriage should be led by hand; but these good orders are not observed.'

There was plenty of poverty and disease as well as evil-doing to be found only just beneath the smiling surface of Elizabethan life. Rat-haunted slums, where the plague erupted every ten years or so, festered alongside the elegant mansions, luxury shops and bulging warehouses, and the lot of the faceless urban poor was probably even worse than that of their country cousins.
All the same, for the well-to-do, the enterprising and the fortunate, life, by

King Philip II of Spain, leader of the European
Catholic powers, Elizabeth's former brother-in-law,
one-time suitor and life-long adversary

4

contemporary standards, was good in Elizabeth Tudor's England. At a time when so much of Western Europe was being ravaged by war, this Protestant island had become the envy of very many Western Europeans.

The Catholic Threat

In 1588 England had been at peace for almost thirty years. 'God gave us Queen Elizabeth,' exclaimed Bishop John Jewel, 'and with her gave us peace, and so long a peace as England hath seldom seen.' But that peace was coming to an end and the year '88 opened with reminders of 'an old and common prophecy' that it would see 'either a marvellous, fearful and horrible alteration of empires and kingdoms' with such 'accidents' as hunger, pestilence, treasons and commotions; even that 'an utter and final over-throw and destruction of the whole world' would ensue.

The good Protestant people of England had no doubt about what this doomful prediction was referring to. Nearly twenty years before, the Pope, misled by inaccurate information about the strength of the surviving English Catholic minority and despairing of a peaceful reconciliation with the English establishment, had issued a bull—*Regnans in Excelsis*—excommunicating Elizabeth 'the pretended Queen of England and Servant of Wickedness.' Elizabeth, the Pope had declared, was not merely 'an Heretick and Favourer of Hereticks' who deserved to be cut off from the unity of the body of Christ, but a bastard and a usurper to be deprived of her pretended title to the kingdom of England. Her subjects were therefore released from their duty of allegiance and positively commanded not to obey the Queen or her laws on pain of inclusion in 'the like sentence of anathema.'

Not surprisingly this papal broadside had provoked angry reaction in England and an upsurge of patriotic anti-Roman, anti-Catholic fervour among the Protestant population. The government had dismissed the bull as 'a vain crack of words that made a noise only,' but the dread remained that one day the European Catholic powers would combine to try to enforce the papal sanctions, and in 1588 that dread had become a reality, as England faced the threat of invasion by the greatest Catholic power of them all.

Philip II, King of Spain, Portugal and Sicily, Lord of the Netherlands and of the rich and wondrous lands of Spain's transatlantic empire, was by common consent the greatest prince in Christendom. He was also nursing a number of longstanding grievances against Queen Elizabeth's England. For example, the English had always refused to accept Spain's jealously guarded monopoly of the lucrative West Indian trade. Denied the opportunity of doing business legitimately, English privateers—or pirates—roamed the Caribbean, raiding Spanish settlements and depots, attacking and plundering the Spanish treasure fleets carrying the annual tribute of gold, silver and precious stones from the mines of Peru, and generally doing their best to 'annoy' the King of Spain with the Queen of England's tacit approval. As well as this, England had for some time been giving aid and encouragement to the Dutch Protestants in

Robert Dudley, Earl of Leicester, the Queen's favourite, 'her brother and best friend,' and, so many believed, the only man she ever seriously considered as a husband. Leicester was commander of the land forces in the Armada campaign. The Queen's visit to Tilbury was his idea and as it turned out it was to be the last time he escorted Elizabeth on a public occasion. He died at Rycote in Oxfordshire in September 1588

The National Portrait Gallery, London

their long and bitter revolt against Spanish rule. In fact, by 1588 an English expeditionary force was fighting side by side with the Dutch and a state of open, if undeclared, war already existed.

The religious aspect of the conflict can easily be exaggerated, but Philip of Spain, that most committed of Catholics, undoubtedly felt a special responsibility towards English Catholics. He had, after all, once spent a year in England as the husband of sad Queen Mary Tudor, who had tried so disastrously to lead her people back into the Roman church.

The King of Spain had been contemplating the possibility of an invasion—the Enterprise of England as it was cautiously referred to in diplomatic correspondence—for a number of years, years during which, it must be admitted, he had been offered steadily increasing provocation. But in the end it was the execution in February 1587 of Mary Queen of Scots, Queen Elizabeth's cousin, heiress and arch-rival, which galvanised him into action against his former sister-in-law.

In public, Philip spoke of his grief at the death of the Queen of Scots who had been so good a Catholic and would have been 'so appropriate an instrument for converting the kingdoms of England and Scotland to our Holy Catholic Faith.' In private, however, the King had always been less than enthused by the prospect of seeing the half-French Mary Stuart on the English throne and would certainly have been more than reluctant to launch an attack which, if successful, could have resulted only in a dramatic increase in the power and influence of France. Soon, though, the situation looked rather different, for, as he wrote to his ambassador in Rome, 'failing the Queen of Scotland, the right to the English crown falls to me. My claim … rests upon my descent from the House of Lancaster, and upon the Will made by the Queen of Scotland.' Not that Philip had any intention of adding England to his own dominions. Instead he meant to settle the crown on his daughter, the Infanta Isabella.

The Armada

Plans and preparations

All through the year of 1587 reports came in of a great fleet being assembled on the coast of the Iberian peninsula. From Andalusia to the Bay of Biscay the work of preparing the Most Happy Armada had begun. There were more than sixty fighting ships—galleons and armed merchantmen—several of them: the *San Martin*, the *San Juan*, *El Gran Grin*, and *Nuestra Señora del Rosario* around the 1000 ton mark. The *San Francisco*, the *Duquesa Santa Ana*, the *San Bartolomeo* and the *Florencia* were all above 900 tons; the *San Luis*, the *San Felipe*, *San Marcos*, *San Mateo*, *Santa Ana* and *San Cristobal* above 750 tons. After the galleons came the *urcas*—the hulks or supply ships—carrying what was hoped would be enough tunny fish, salt beef and bacon, biscuit, dried peas and beans, rice, cheese, garlic, vinegar and wine to last 30 000 men for up to eight months. There were four galleasses—an experimental hybrid of sailing ship and oared vessel—four

A galleass, hybrid of sailing ship and oared vessel. Four of them sailed with the Armada

Walmer Castle, one of a string of coastal forts stretching from Cornwall to Kent, built by Henry VIII to counter the threat of invasion by the Catholic powers during the 1530s and 40s. Walmer, later the official residence of the Lords Warden of the Cinque Ports, was one of the 'Castles in the Downs'

Deal Castle is the largest and most complete of Henry VIII's coastal forts. It was well prepared to carry out its defensive role in 1588 but was not put to the test

actual galleys and a swarm of little ships, the dispatch boats, scouts and message carriers. Altogether the Armada numbered 130 sail, great and small.

The Duke of Medina Sidonia, commander of this mighty force, has always had an undeservedly bad press. It was not, after all, his fault that he had no experience of sea-faring or of war, or that he suffered from seasickness when afloat. Co-opted at the last moment following the death of the veteran Admiral Santa Cruz, Medina Sidonia did his best in what were to become impossibly difficult circumstances. A conscientious, well-meaning and deeply religious man, he was anxious that good order and discipline be maintained in the fleet—especially bearing in mind the quasi-crusading nature of the enterprise—and instructed his officers to take particular care that no soldier or sailor embarking on the Armada 'shall blaspheme or deny Our Lord, Our Lady or the Saints.' Gambling was to be discouraged as much as possible and no women were to be taken on board. In order to avoid the possibility of injury or death if quarrels broke out, no man was to carry a dagger. All were to obey their officers and the soldiers were to allow the rations to be given out by those in charge and not attempt to take them by force.

The Armada was not expected to undertake the conquest and conversion of England by itself. In fact, contrary to generally held belief, it was not intended to undertake the conquest of England at all. Its orders were to rendezvous with the Duke of Parma, commander-in-chief of Spanish land forces in the Netherlands, and to escort the army as it crossed the Channel in a fleet of barges then being assembled at Dunkirk. (A strikingly similar notion was to occur in later centuries to other would-be invaders—to Napoleon Bonaparte and Adolf Hitler for example.) King Philip, writing to the Duke of Parma, made it all sound very simple. The Armada, Parma was informed, would anchor 'off Margate Point.' Whereupon, seeing his passage assured by the arrival of the fleet, the Duke of Parma was to be ready, weather permitting, to cross with his whole army. Until this had been accomplished the Armada was not to attempt a landing on the English coast and Medina Sidonia was warned specifically not to allow himself to be diverted, however strong the provocation. 'The success of the business depends upon our striking at the root,' wrote Philip. 'You will not be deflected from your course, but will continue straight on without seeking the enemy.'

St Mawes Castle, which faces Pendennis Castle across the mile-wide entrance to the inlet of Carrick Roads east of Falmouth

The Armada sets sail

The Armada sailed from Lisbon on 18 May 1588, but the weather was bad and so many alarming defects and deficiencies were discovered that the fleet was forced to put in at Corunna on the northwest coast of Spain to revictual and refit. Finally, on 12 July, it set sail once more, as ready as it would ever be. It was an enormous, awesome undertaking; nothing on such a scale had ever been attempted before.

> *The Spanish fleet did flote in narrow Seas,*
> *And bend her Ships against the English shore,*
> *With so great rage as nothing could appease,*
> *And with such strength as never seen before.*

Calshot Castle, built in 1539-40, faces the Isle of Wight and guards the entrance to Southampton Water. It was repaired and strengthened to meet the renewed threat of invasion in the 1580s and again during the Napoleonic Wars and was manned as recently as the Second World War

Pendennis Castle, one of a pair with St Mawes, was built in the early 1540s to guard the entrance to Carrick Roads and the River Fal. Both castles were planned as artillery forts and their squat rounded forms are typical of Henry VIII's castles of this period. In 1583 and again in 1591 Pendennis Castle was repaired and put in readiness to meet the threat from the sea and, like many other Tudor fortresses, was manned up to and including the Second World War

Drake's Warning

The Spanish fleet might have floated in the narrow seas a year earlier had it not been for the intervention of Sir Francis Drake, the most renowned of the Elizabethan 'sea dogs'. To the Spaniards Drake was a bogeyman, a corsair and a common pirate. He was the dreaded El Draque, a wizard who kept a magic mirror in his cabin enabling him to see over the horizon. To the English he was a national hero, although his arrogance and tendency to 'vaingloriousness' helped to make him enemies in high places.

Himself an implacable enemy of Spain and Rome and everything they stood for, Drake was a prodigy, a restless thrustful genius, totally convinced of the justice of the Protestant cause and his own God-given mission to uphold it. He was convinced, too, that attack was the best means of defence and constantly urged on a cautious government the tactical wisdom of the pre-emptive strike. 'The advantage of time and place in all martial actions is half a victory.' In the spring of 1587 he got his way and led a small naval task force in a brilliantly successful smash-and-grab raid on the crowded anchorage at Cadiz, destroying some 10 000 tons of shipping intended for the Armada. This, the so-called 'Singeing of the King of Spain's Beard,' had seriously delayed Philip's preparations and confirmed all Drake's worst fears about their extent. In fact, he had hardly dared to write of the great forces which the King of Spain was gathering and added the urgent warning: 'Prepare in England strongly and most by sea.'

The raid on Cadiz when Drake 'singed the King of Spain's beard' and delayed the sailing of the Armada by at least a year

The English Navy Royal

England was preparing by sea, thanks very largely to the vision and dedication of John Hawkins, Treasurer of the Navy Board. During his period in office Hawkins set himself to root out the corruption and pilfering which he found at every level in the royal dockyards. More important still, he committed himself to sponsoring a far-reaching programme of building and rebuilding the royal ships to revolutionary modern designs.

In pre-Hawkins days it had been customary to regard the warship as little more than a floating platform for carrying artillery and soldiers, the purpose of which was to grapple with and board the enemy. The fighting ship armed with heavy guns capable of firing broadside was a new development in naval warfare and one in which English naval architects and shipwrights such as Matthew Baker and Peter Pett were taking the lead. The traditional top-heavy, tub-shaped galleons had their towering forecastles and sterncastles lowered, and new vessels were built on sleeker lines with less freeboard and a longer keel in proportion to their beam, giving them greater speed and manoeuvrability.

The result was that the English Navy Royal now contained some of the most

Dartmouth Castle guarding the entrance to the River Dart

The Lord Admiral, Charles Howard of Effingham.
Although not a professional seaman he genuinely
loved the navy and the company of those noble ships.
He also did his best after the battle for the sailors who
were dying of typhus on the streets of Margate and
other ports in the southeast: 'It would grieve any
man's heart to see them that have served so valiantly
to die so miserably'

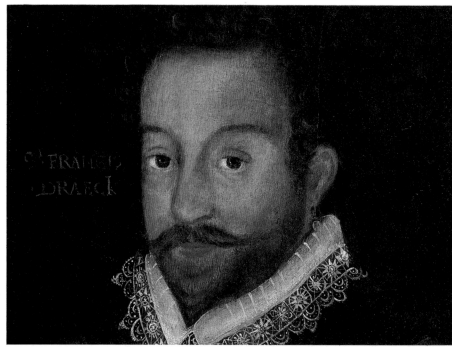

Francis Drake, seaman extraordinary, the most
internationally famous Englishman of his times.
A man of 'medium stature, blond, rather heavy than
slender, merry, careful … well spoken, inclined to
liberality and to ambition, vainglorious, boastful, not
very cruel'

formidable warships afloat and by the beginning of 1588 the whole force of some thirty-four ships, large and small, had been brought to a peak of readiness. When the great galleons were beached in the spring tides to be scraped and tallowed William Hawkins, Mayor of Plymouth, could tell brother John: 'The ships sit aground so strongly and are so staunch as if they were made of a whole tree.' The Lord Admiral, Charles Howard of Effingham, on inspecting his command, was equally happy to report that 'I have been aboard of every ship that goeth out with me and in every place where any may creep and I do thank God that they be in the estate they are; for there is never a one of them that knows what a leak means.'

While the names of Drake and Hawkins, Walter Raleigh and Martin Frobisher come readily to mind when thinking of Elizabethan seafarers, that of Charles Howard is rather less familiar. But it was he, as Lord High Admiral of England, who was entrusted with the responsibility of overall command of the fleet. A member of the influential Howard clan and thus related to the Queen on her mother's side, he possessed the authority—very necessary in an intensely status-conscious age—conferred by aristocratic rank. Fortunately he also possessed the equally valuable qualities of tact, fairness and firmness which earned him the respect of that rugged band of individualists gathered to fight the Spaniards in that fateful summer of 1588. Charles Howard was not a professional seaman, but he truly loved the navy: 'If it were not for her Majesty's presence, I had rather live in the company of these noble ships than in any other place.' He showed a genuine, conscientious concern for the men under his command.

Martin Frobisher who commanded the *Triumph*, the largest galleon in either fleet

Life on board ship

Conditions of life for the rank and file on board an Elizabethan sea-going ship were extremely uncomfortable, over-crowded and insanitary. Although efforts were made to take on fresh food whenever possible, the sailors' ordinary diet consisted chiefly of salt beef and pork, salt fish, ship's biscuit, wine and beer. In theory, each man and boy was allowed a pound of biscuit and a gallon of beer per day, with a pound of beef or pork and peas on Sunday, Monday, Tuesday and Thursday, and on other days of the week a side of salt fish to every mess of four men. In practice, however, food on board ship, especially on a long voyage, was often in very short supply and often bad. Drinking water, stored in wooden casks, quickly became foul and victuallers were well known for their habit of charging top prices for putrid meat, stale beer and maggoty biscuit. No wonder disease was rampant. Dysentery, typhus and scurvy all took their toll—scurvy in particular, that 'plague of the sea and spoil of mariners,' was estimated to have killed 10 000 sailors in the space of twenty years; it was not unusual for at least half a ship's crew to die during a voyage. An Elizabethan sailing ship was a labour-intensive machine and a big galleon would carry a crew of several hundred, but even so some vessels were lost because there were just not enough men left alive to bring them back to port.

The royal ships were not kept permanently at sea—that would have been impossibly expensive. Except in time of national emergency, or when they were

Ark Royal, Charles Howard's flagship in the Armada battle

needed for some special service, they were laid up in harbour and their crews paid off. But by late May 1588 the whole fleet was in commission and the Lord Admiral with a squadron (led by the *Ark Raleigh*—later the *Ark Royal*, the *Triumph*, the *Elizabeth Jonas*, the *Bear*, the *Victory*, the *Elizabeth Bonaventure*, *Lion*, *Dreadnought* and *Vanguard*) had sailed from the Medway to join forces with the West Country contingent, commanded by Francis Drake in the *Revenge* and based at Plymouth. Drake was to be vice-admiral of the combined fleet and Howard's chief of staff. Distinguished though Drake was it would have been impossible to give him supreme command without arousing dangerous jealousy among his fellow captains. It is to his credit that he accepted the subordinate position with good grace.

Like the King of Spain, Queen Elizabeth relied heavily on the armed merchantmen supplied by her principal seaports (the City of London contributed twenty ships) and even by private individuals such as Walter Raleigh and the Earl of Leicester to make up her naval strength. Of the ninety odd ships mustered at Plymouth to await the Spanish attack only nineteen actually belonged to the Crown.

The crews of these ships were fretting to get to grips with the enemy. 'I would to God the Prince of Parma were upon the seas with all his forces and we in the view of them,' wrote William Wynter who, with Sir Henry Seymour, had been left to guard the Straits of Dover. Down in the West Country, too, morale was high, and Drake and Howard were able to assure the Queen that neither of them had ever known better men, possessed of 'gallanter minds,' than the captains, soldiers and mariners voluntarily gathered together to put their hands and hearts to the business of finishing off the Spaniards.

There were problems. The weather was terrible—'here is such weat her as never was seen at this time of year'—and a succession of southwesterly gales was keeping the fleet penned up in the haven at Plymouth. Charles Howard was also seriously worried about the supply situation and the difficulties he was experiencing in feeding his gallant company. It seemed especially shocking that men so desirous to spend their lives in the service of their country should lack meat. But in spite of repeated complaints by the Lord Admiral and his officers the efforts of the commissariat continued to leave much to be desired. Marmaduke Darell, the harassed official in charge of victualling the fleet, was doing his best, but the basic administrative machinery, the transport, storage space, and facilities for baking and brewing necessary for supplying so large a number over so long a period of time simply did not exist. With the best will in the world Darell's task was an impossible one, and in the end he was reduced to going round the neighbourhood with a shopping basket, picking up any food he could get his hands on.

The weeks passed. June turned into July and still the waiting continued. Howard began to wonder if the Spaniards meant 'nothing else but to linger it out upon their own coast until … we have spent our victuals here.' Francis Drake, frustrated by official caution and contrary winds, was still pressing for permission to proceed to sea and 'hinder' the Armada's quiet passage into England.

Shipwrights at the royal dockyard, Chatham,
Matthew Baker and Peter Pett, who were largely
responsible, under the direction of John Hawkins,
for building and rebuilding the Queen's ships to new
designs which enabled them to outsail and outgun
the Armada

English man of war, 1588, which shows the new
design of warship, longer, lower and thus faster and
more manoeuvrable

The Armada is sighted

At last, on the afternoon of Friday 19 July, Captain Thomas Fleming of the bark *Golden Hind*, brought the news to Plymouth that the Spanish fleet had been sighted that morning off the Isles of Scilly. According to the traditional story—which first appeared in print in 1624—Fleming found the Lord Admiral and a group of his senior officers playing bowls on Plymouth Hoe; this was the occasion when Francis Drake is said to have remarked: 'Time enough to finish the game and beat the Spaniards too.'

Whether this well-known tale is true or not, it is certainly true that there would have been plenty of time to finish a leisurely game of bowls. The wind was still blowing hard from the southwest and the tide flooding into Plymouth Sound. Until the turn of the tide, round about ten o'clock that evening, the English battle fleet was effectively immobilised. All through that night Plymouth harbour seethed with activity as the seamen sweated at the oars of the ships' boats—warping or towing the heavy galleons out on the ebb tide. All through that night, too, beacon fires were flinging the news from hilltop to hilltop—leaping along the south coast from the Lizard to Beachy Head, up to Bristol and South Wales, across the Sussex Downs to the Surrey hills and the heights of Hampstead and on into the Midland shires:

> *Till Belvoir's lordly terraces the sign to Lincoln sent,*
> *And Lincoln sent the message on, o'er the wild vale of Trent;*
> *Till Skiddaw saw the fire that burnt on Gaunt's embattled pile,*
> *And the red glare on Skiddaw roused the burghers of Carlisle.*

The Battle

The two fleets first made visual contact on Saturday 20 July at about three o'clock in the afternoon, and during that night the English succeeded in gaining the advantage of the wind. In other words, they sailed out to sea across the enemy's bows and, by means of a very nice piece of seamanship, worked their way round on to the seaward and windward flank of the advancing Armada. This not merely demonstrated the sailing qualities of the ships and expertise of their crews, but gave the English the crucial advantage of freedom of movement—allowing them to pursue the Spaniards up the Channel, pick off any stragglers and to a large extent dictate the conduct of the battle.

All the same, the English were not complacent. The sheer size of the Armada and the obvious defensive strength of its crescent-shaped formation were enough to make any sensible opponent cautious. After their first encounter on Sunday 21 July, Howard reported that although some damage had been inflicted on the enemy, 'we durst not adventure to put in among them, their fleet being so strong.'

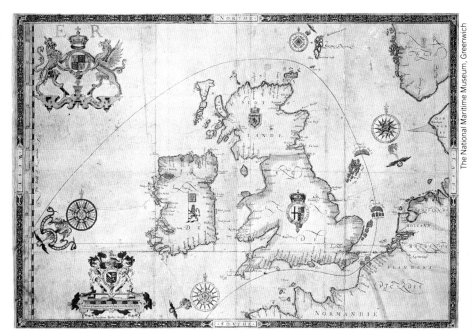

Armada map. After the defeat at Gravelines the Armada ran northwards before the wind and, as it vanished into the mists round the north of Scotland, Europe buzzed with rumours of its whereabouts. Many believed it would reappear at any moment and renew the attack

THE NORTH EAST VIEW OF PENDENNIS CASTLE, IN THE COUNTY OF CORNWALL.

THIS CASTLE of Pendennis or Pendinas, stands on a Peninsula; it is large and well fortify'd, built by K. Hen. 8. for the Defence of Falmouth Harbour. Q. Eliz: added considerably to the Fortifications. It held out a long Time for K. Cha: 1. but after a Strait Siege, it was forced to Surrender to the Parliament Forces.

Northeast view of Pendennis Castle from an engraving by Samuel and Nathaniel Buck

On the following day the Armada lost two capital ships, though neither as a result of the fighting. One, *Nuestra Señora del Rosario*, lost her rudder and had to be abandoned. The other, the *San Salvador*, 'a great Biscayan of 800 tons or thereabouts,' blew up after the fire started in her magazine.

On Tuesday, day three of the fight in the Channel, the wind veered. The English temporarily lost the weather advantage and a somewhat confused battle took place off Portland Bill, the English trying to recover the wind, the Spaniards trying to close with their irritatingly nimble adversaries. While this was going on, Martin Frobisher in the *Triumph* (the biggest ship in either fleet), with five middle-sized London ships, became separated from the main body and was attacked by Don Hugo de Moncada's galleasses. Whether Frobisher was really in trouble or simply trying to lure the galleasses into a trap is not very clear, but as the wind shifted again to the southwest Howard in the *Ark Royal*, followed by the *Elizabeth Jonas*, the *Galleon of Leicester*, the *Golden Lion*, the *Victory*, the *Mary Rose*, the *Dreadnought* and the *Swallow* went hurrying to the rescue, 'which the Duke of Medina perceiving, came out with sixteen of his best galleons to impeach his lordship and stop him from assisting the *Triumph*. At which assault, after wonderful sharp conflict, the Spaniards were forced to give way and to flock together like sheep.'

After this, apart from an indecisive skirmish off the Isle of Wight on the Thursday, there was a lull in the fighting. The English ships had been using up their ammunition at a quite unprecedented rate and were obliged to send urgently to Portsmouth 'for a new supply of such provisions.' The Justices of the Peace and captains of the forts and castles along the south coast responded with reinforcements of men, powder and shot, victuals and ships, but the Armada, which was also running short of powder and shot, had no ready source of supply—not, that is, until it made contact with the Duke of Parma.

On the evening of Saturday 27 July, the Spanish fleet 'came near unto Calais on the coast of Picardy' and there, said Charles Howard, 'suddenly came to an anchor over against the cliffs of Calais, and our English fleet anchored short of them, within culverin shot of the enemy. This was the moment when, if things had gone according to plan, the Duke of Parma's army should have put out from Dunkirk in flat-bottomed boats, ready to cross the Channel escorted by the Invincible Armada. But no one appears to have told the King of Spain that Parma's army was effectively blockaded by the Dutch fleet, and the Armada dared not approach too close to the treacherous shoals and sandbanks of the Flanders coast. The plan which had looked so simple on paper was a practical impossibility. Meanwhile, the Armada, with no deep-water port where it could go for shelter or take on urgently needed supplies of food and ammunition, would soon be in serious difficulties. The Duke of Medina Sidonia knew this only too well. 'I am now at anchor two leagues from Calais, the enemy's fleet being on my flank, whilst I am not in a position to do him much harm,' he told Parma in an attempt to explain his predicament.

The English had had the best of the action so far, but the running fight in the Channel had not settled anything; the English fleet had not been able to break the Armada's defensive formation and Charles Howard and his senior officers did not trust the Dutch to keep Parma at bay—they feared he might suddenly

The Armada Portrait of Queen Elizabeth with one hand covering the globe, and the crown beside her. Behind her two panels display the advance of the dreaded Spanish fleet and its humiliating defeat at the hands of her navy

19

emerge and keep his rendezvous with Medina Sidonia after all. On Sunday 28 July it was decided that the Armada must be flushed out of Calais Roads without further delay. The obvious way to achieve this was by means of fire-ships and late that night eight small vessels filled with combustible material, their guns loaded 'and having the wind and tide with them' were set alight and 'let drive among the Spanish fleet.'

Fire was one of the greatest dangers a wooden sailing ship had to fear and panic swept through the crowded anchorage as the Armada captains cut their cables and scrambled out to sea in the darkness. The fireships had succeeded in breaking the formidable Spanish discipline but by morning the scattered ships had rallied, stubbornly reformed 'into the proportion of a half moon' and were once more ready to do battle.

The Battle of Gravelines, which lasted all through that August Monday, was to prove the decisive encounter of the campaign, but Charles Howard was still not claiming anything like a final victory. 'We have chased the Spaniards in fight until this evening late and distressed them much,' he wrote to the Secretary of State, Francis Walsingham, from aboard Her Majesty's ship the *Ark*, 'but their fleet consisteth of mighty ships and great strength.' And he added in a postscript to his report: 'Their force is wonderful great and strong; and yet we pluck their feathers by little and little.' Francis Drake was rather more optimistic: 'God hath given us so good a day in forcing the enemy so far to leeward as I hope the Prince of Parma and the Duke of Sidonia shall not shake hands this few days.'

Dover Castle, guardian of the Straits from Roman times

Victory

During Monday night the wind blew hard from the northwest, driving the unhappy Spaniards relentlessly towards the shoals and banks of the Dutch and Flanders coast. Two ships went aground on the banks off Nieuwpoort and Oostende, and by dawn on Tuesday it looked as if the whole fleet would be pounded to destruction on the Zeeland sands. Then, suddenly, the wind veered again and Drake wrote exultantly to Walsingham, 'there was never anything pleased me better than the seeing the enemy flying with a southerly wind to northward.'

The Spaniards were in a desperate state. Battered by the English broadsides and the weather, they had lost five capital ships in the past four days. Many more were leaking, others had lost spars and rigging and casualties were heavy throughout the fleet. There was hardly any ammunition left and very little food—every man was rationed to eight ounces of biscuit and half a pint of wine a day. There was nothing the unhappy Medina Sidonia could do but try to salvage as much as possible of his defeated and demoralised command, and by the first week of August the Armada was on the first leg of its long painful journey home, right around the coast of Scotland and off the west coast of Ireland. Estimates of its losses vary widely, but it seems about half the original

The launching of the fireships. Fire was one of the greatest hazards to a sixteenth-century ship, with its flammable cordage, timber and sails. Fireships were small unmanned vessels, filled with pitch and sometimes gunpowder. They would be set alight and allowed to sail with the wind and tide in a crowded anchorage to spread panic through an enemy fleet

The Pevensey Gun. One of two demi-culverins that formed the only armament of Pevensey Castle at the time of the Spanish Armada (the other is now in the Tower of London). It is of iron, and certainly of Sussex Weald manufacture, but the carriage is a modern replica based on contemporary illustrations

ships were lost and about fifty of King Philip's galleons eventually succeeded in limping back to the ports of northern Spain.

The English kept up their pursuit as far as the mouth of the Tyne, but on 2 August the bulk of the fleet turned back and began dropping anchor at Harwich, Margate Roads and other southeast ports. Food by this time was running very low and an epidemic of typhus was raging through the ships. 'It is a most pitiful sight to see here at Margate how the men, having no place to receive them, die in the streets,' wrote the compassionate Lord Admiral. 'I am driven myself of force to come on land, to see them bestowed in some lodging; and the best I can get is barns and such outhouses; and the relief is small that I can provide for them.' Charles Howard's heart was grieved to see 'them that have served so valiantly to die so miserably,' but this sort of tragedy was an inescapable part of sixteenth-century life. Again, in the England of Elizabeth I, the resources for dealing with such a situation simply did not exist and, after the fashion of the times, 'the great cause of this infection amongst us' was attributed to the bad beer. 'For my own part,' sighed Howard, 'I know not which way to deal with the mariners to make them rest contented with sour beer, for nothing doth displease them more.'

As was usually the case in such circumstances, sickness continued to claim more victims than any killed in battle but there could be no question of immediate demobilisation.

Queen Elizabeth at Tilbury

No one on shore had any idea of the magnitude of the victory when Queen Elizabeth paid her famous visit to Tilbury to review the citizen army camped around Stratford, East Ham and other villages to the east of London. Tilbury was the headquarters of the Queen's land forces.

The Queen came down the Thames from Westminster in the royal barge with 'trumpets sounding and dubbing drums apace' and was greeted at Tilbury by a salvo of cannon fired from the fort. The visit, which had been suggested by the Earl of Leicester, commander-in-chief of the land forces, as a morale booster for the troops, proved a triumphant success. 'The Queen with a masculine spirit came and took a view of her Army and Camp at Tilbury,' wrote the contemporary historian William Camden, 'and riding about through the ranks of armed men with a leader's truncheon in her hand, sometimes with a martial pace, another while gently like a woman, incredible it is how much she encouraged the hearts of her soldiers by her presence and speech to them ....'

The Queen, too, undoubtedly enjoyed herself. With her instinctive flair for an occasion she had dismissed her bodyguard, declaring that she did not desire to live to distrust her faithful and loving people. Such fear was for tyrants. She had always so behaved herself that, under God, she placed her strength and her safety in the loyal hearts and goodwill of her subjects. And her faithful loving subjects responded joyfully. They did not see a thin elderly woman

Bridgeman Art Library

Queen Elizabeth, shining in her favourite white and silver, being carried shoulder high by her courtiers. The Gentlemen Pensioners, the royal bodyguard, line her route and the ladies of honour follow Her Majesty. This is Elizabeth as Gloriana and virgin goddess

(Elizabeth was approaching her fifty-fifth birthday) with bad teeth, wearing an improbable red wig and perched up on the back of a large white horse. Instead they saw, through a golden haze of emotional patriotism, the personification of every classical goddess, every biblical heroine from Judith and Deborah to Diana the Huntress and the Queen of the Amazons. And, of course, 'the Goddess of the land,' their own peerless Queen whom 'all there then did jointly love and fear.'

It was in this highly charged atmosphere that Elizabeth made her great Tilbury Speech. She had come, she told her soldiers, being resolved to live or die amongst them all, 'to lay down for my God and for my Kingdom and for my people my honour and my blood even in the dust.' And she went on: 'I know I have the body but of a weak and feeble woman; but I have the heart and stomach of a King, and of a King of England too, and think foul scorn that Parma or Spain or any Prince of Europe should dare to invade the borders of my Realm; to which, rather than any dishonour shall grow by me, I myself will take up arms….'

Small wonder, in the circumstances, that her audience rose to her with 'a mighty shout,' and when the Queen had gone back to London, perhaps a little disappointed that she had not, after all, been called upon to take up arms herself, the Earl of Leicester wrote to the Earl of Shrewsbury: 'Our gracious mistress hath been here with me to see her camp and people, which so enflamed the hearts of her good subjects, as I think the weakest person among them is able to match the proudest Spaniard that dares land in England.'

The year 1588, which saw a small island—only half the island in fact—defy and repulse the onslaught of the greatest power in Europe, marked the high noon of the Elizabethan epic, and the story of the Spanish Armada, with all its attendant myths and legends, has become a much loved and valued part of English history and folklore. But it is worth bearing in mind how narrow the margin of safety actually was—a mile or so of sand and mudbank at the mouth of the Scheldt estuary. If the entrance to the Scheldt and the deep-water port of Flushing had not been guarded by the Dutch fleet, the so-called Sea Beggars, and a small English garrison; if the Prince of Parma and the Duke of Sidonia *had* succeeded in shaking hands and Parma's dreaded army of battle-hardened Blackbeards been able to make a landing on English soil, then the story might have had a very different ending.

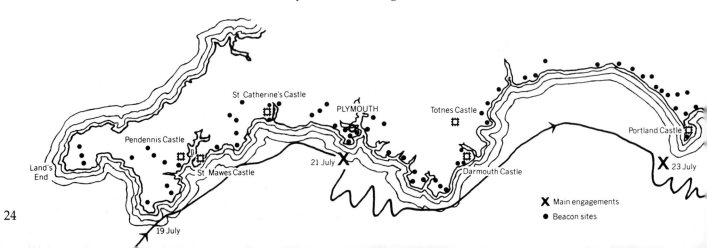